Surviving History

THE SEARCH FOR EL DORADO

Virginia Loh-Hagan

45TH PARALLEL PRESS

Published in the United States of America by Cherry Lake Publishing Group
Ann Arbor, Michigan
www.cherrylakepublishing.com

Reading Adviser: Marla Conn, MS, Ed., Literacy specialist, Read-Ability, Inc.
Book Designer: Melinda Millward

Photo Credits: © Kanea/Adobe Stock, front cover, 1; © Caroline.blackburn/Shutterstock.com, 4; © tbradford/iStock.com, 6; © Oyls/Shutterstock.com, 8; © Morphart Creation/Shutterstock.com, 10; © Dr Morley Read/Shutterstock.com, 12; © Nika Lerman/Shutterstock.com, 14; © Sutra Communication/ Shutterstock.com, 16; © OscarSurmano/Shutterstock.com, 18; © Destinyweddingstudio/Shutterstock. com, 20; © Vladimir Wrangel/Shutterstock.com, 22, back cover; © Toniflap/Shutterstock.com, 24; © Ammit Jack/Shutterstock.com, 27; © Iryna Savina/Shutterstock.com, 28

Graphic Element Credits: © Milos Djapovic/Shutterstock.com, back cover, front cover; © cajoer/ Shutterstock.com, back cover, front cover, multiple interior pages; © GUSAK OLENA/Shutterstock.com, back cover, multiple interior pages; © Miloje/Shutterstock.com, front cover; © Rtstudio/Shutterstock. com, multiple interior pages; © Konstantin Nikiteev/Dreamstime.com, 29

Library of Congress Cataloging-in-Publication Data

Names: Loh-Hagan, Virginia, author.
Title: The search for El Dorado / by Virginia Loh-Hagan.
Description: Ann Arbor, Michigan : Cherry Lake Publishing, [2021] | Series:
    Surviving history | Includes index.
Identifiers: LCCN 2020030322 (print) | LCCN 2020030323 (ebook) | ISBN 9781534180314 (hardcover)|
    ISBN 9781534182028 (paperback) | ISBN 9781534181328 (pdf) | ISBN 9781534183032 (ebook)
Subjects: LCSH: America—Discovery and exploration—Juvenile literature. | El Dorado—Juvenile literature.
Classification: LCC E121 .L64 2021 (print) | LCC E121 (ebook) | DDC 970.01—dc23
LC record available at https://lccn.loc.gov/2020030322
LC ebook record available at https://lccn.loc.gov/2020030323

Cherry Lake Publishing Group would like to acknowledge the work of the Partnership for 21st Century
Learning, a Network of Battelle for Kids. Please visit http://www.battelleforkids.org/networks/p21
for more information.

Printed in the United States of America
Corporate Graphics

TABLE OF CONTENTS

INTRODUCTION

In the El Dorado legend, gold and gems were believed to have been thrown into the lake as an offering to an underwater god.

El Dorado is the lost city of gold. It's a **legend**. Legends are stories that some people believe to be true. The El Dorado legend started around the 1530s. Spanish explorers **conquered** parts of South America. Conquer means to take control. They heard stories about a king covered in gold dust. They heard stories about a city made of gold.

Many people have lost their lives looking for El Dorado. They were lost in the jungles. They were killed by local tribes. They **starved**. Starve means to die of hunger. They got sick. But that didn't stop many explorers from still searching. They wanted to find the gold. The most famous explorer was Sir Walter Raleigh. Raleigh was English. He made two trips to find El Dorado. He saw one of his men get eaten by a crocodile. Another one of his men **disappeared**. Disappeared means vanished.

The Andes are among the world's longest mountain ranges.

El Dorado is believed to be near the Andes Mountains. This is a harsh area. There are many dangers. Explorers would have to survive the mountains. They'd have to survive the Amazon River. They'd have to survive the Amazon **rainforest**. A rainforest is an area of thick trees. It has a lot of rainfall. It has many dangerous animals. It has many poisonous plants. It's also beautiful. It has many different life-forms.

STAY OR GO?

It took several months to get ready for an expedition.

Between 1530 and 1650, thousands of men searched for El Dorado. They went into unexplored areas of the Amazon. They risked their lives. They wanted fame. They wanted riches.

Expeditions are journeys or adventures. El Dorado expedition leaders needed a lot of money. They had to buy supplies. The first expeditions started in a coastal city in South America. Between 100 and 700 men joined. **Enslaved** people were forced to join expeditions. An enslaved person is someone who is owned by another person and forced to work for free. They had to carry supplies.

Expeditions could last months or years. During this time, many men died. Some got sick. Some left. Expeditions ended when supplies and men became low.

QUESTION 1

Would you have gone on an expedition?

A You were a woman. Not many women at the time had the opportunity to go on expeditions. The expeditions were considered too dangerous.

B You were a rich man. You could pay for your own armor, weapons, and horses. You could also bring along hogs. You ate the hogs along the way. You got a big share of the treasures.

C You were a poor man. You joined as a worker. You got a small share of the treasures. You had no supplies of your own. You had to rely on the expedition leader.

Some expedition leaders brought fighting dogs. These dogs were used to defend against attackers.

SURVIVOR BIOGRAPHY

Antonio de Berrio lived from 1527 to 1596. He was a
Spanish soldier. He joined the military at age 14. He was
appointed governor of a city in the Americas. He began
searching for El Dorado. His first expedition was in 1584.
He had 80 men. He was stopped by the rainy season. His
second expedition was in 1587. This lasted over 2 years.
His third expedition was in 1590. During this expedition,
his wife died. Berrio spent most of his money. He asked the
Spanish king for more money. The king sent him 300 men
and supplies. In 1595, he met Sir Walter Raleigh. Raleigh
wanted to find El Dorado as well. Raleigh attacked. He
took Berrio as a prisoner. He forced Berrio to be his guide.
Berrio took them to the areas he already explored. He was
freed later that year. When he died, his son continued his
search for El Dorado.

TAN OR BURN?

Rainforests have 4 layers: the emergent, the canopy, the understory, and the ground layer. The emergent layer is at the top. It gets the most sun.

Most of the El Dorado explorers were from Europe. They had pale skin. They suffered under the harsh sun. Within hours, the men's skin burned. This was very painful. Sunburns can lead to **blisters**. Blisters are bubbles on the skin. They're sores. They can lead to scars.

The Amazon rainforest is rainy and hot. This is great for plants. But it's not great for humans. The weather is always **humid**. Humid means having a lot of water in the air. The weather made the men weak. They couldn't work as much. They tired easily. They had a hard time breathing.

QUESTION 2

How would you have protected yourself from the sun?

A You were rich. You had enslaved workers to carry shade for you. You wore long sleeves. You wore long pants. You had extra clothes.

B You had some money. You weren't rich or poor. You wore hats. You wore cloth over your face.

C You were poor. You found mud or clay. You rubbed it on your face. You did this as often as you could.

The wet season lasts from October to May. There are especially heavy rains in March and April.

SURVIVAL BY THE NUMBERS

- Over 90 percent of the Amazon people were wiped out during the peak of Amazonian exploration.
- The Amazon rainforest is located in 9 countries.
- About 20 million to 30 million people live in the Amazon rainforest. They depend on the rainforest for survival.
- About 1/5 of the world's freshwater is in the Amazon Basin. Basins are dips in the Earth's surface.
- The Amazon rainforest stores over 180 billion tons of carbon. When trees are cleared or burned, that carbon is released into the air.
- In the last 30 to 40 years, the Amazon has lost about 20 percent of its forests. This is more than has been lost in the past 450 years.
- A 4 mile area (6.4 kilometers) of rainforest has about 1,500 flowering plants, 750 species of trees, 400 species of birds, and 150 species of butterflies. Species means animal groups.
- Rainforests cover less than 6 percent of Earth's total surface area. Yet they're home to 50 percent of Earth's plants and animals.

HEALTHY OR SICK?

Many Amazon rainforest plants are poisonous.

The Amazon rainforest was a new environment. The El Dorado explorers weren't used to it. Many of them got sick.

The biggest dangers were mosquitoes. Mosquitoes carried malaria and yellow fever. These are deadly illnesses. They cause fevers. They cause aches and pains. They cause vomiting.

Explorers also got sick from the food and water. Their stomachs weren't used to the food and water. They could get fevers. They could get **dehydrated**. Dehydrated means lacking water.

QUESTION 3

How would you have protected yourself from mosquito bites?

A You found plants that repel mosquitoes. You rubbed the plant oils on your skin. You made a **smudge** with the dried plants. Smudges are fires that make smoke. They burn slowly.

B You covered up at night. You used a net for sleeping. Mosquitoes bite all day. But they're most active at night.

C You wore light clothing. Mosquitoes hone in on color contrast. They seek dark colors that stand out.

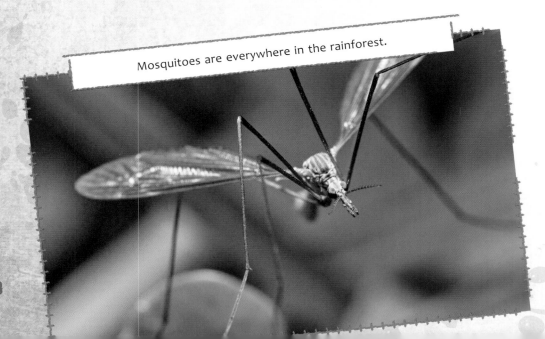

Mosquitoes are everywhere in the rainforest.

SURVIVAL TIPS

Follow these tips to survive the Amazon jungle:

- Cover your skin. Wear pants. Wear long sleeves. Avoid bug bites. Avoid sunburn.
- Get water. Look for groups of bugs. This usually means water is nearby.
- Never wear wet socks. Feet can get infected.
- Walk downhill. Going downhill can lead to water.
- Leave a trail. Make markers from torn clothing.
- Look for gaps in the forest.
- Save your energy. Make slow and steady movements.
- Don't grab any vines or plants. They may have thorns.
- Only eat foods you know.
- Use a compass and map. Stars may be covered by the trees.
- Pick your feet up from the ground. Avoid tripping over roots.
- Take shelter on the highest ground possible.
- Always check your boots or shoes. Make sure no animals have crawled inside.

PREDATOR OR PREY?

Most predators are **nocturnal**.
Nocturnal means they hunt at night.

The Amazon rainforest is full of dangerous **predators**. Predators are hunters. The El Dorado explorers had never seen such beasts.

Bushmaster pit vipers are long, **venomous** snakes. Venom is poison that's injected by fangs. These vipers are 10 feet (3 meters) long. They can bite several times.

Anacondas are snakes. They're up to 30 feet (9.1 m) long. They can weigh up to 100 pounds (45 kilograms). They squeeze their **prey** to death. Prey are animals that are hunted.

Poison dart frogs are brightly colored. They're 1 inch (2.5 centimeters) long. A golden poison frog has enough poison to kill 10,000 mice or 10 men.

Jaguars are big cats. They have sharp claws. They have strong jaws. They can crush skulls.

QUESTION 4

How would you shelter yourself at night?

A You camped with other people. You cleared the land. You set up tents. You set up fire pits. Fire and smoke could ward off predators.

B You slept in a tree. You slept on a branch. Or you slept in a **hammock**. Hammocks are hanging beds. But some Amazon predators can climb trees. Snakes can climb trees.

C You slept in open air. You didn't have a tent or hammock. You were exposed to nature.

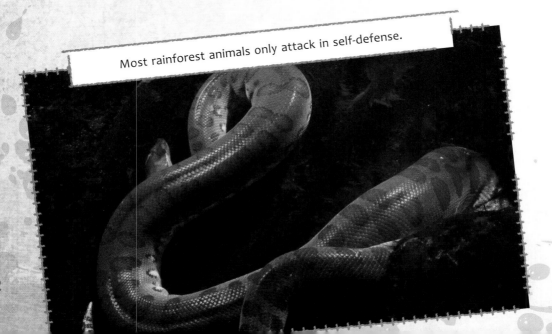

Most rainforest animals only attack in self-defense.

SURVIVAL TOOLS

A machete is an important tool for surviving jungles. Machetes come in all shapes and sizes. They're long knives. They're like swords. Their blades have sharp, jagged edges. They look like saw blades. Chopping is the main purpose of machetes. Machetes are great for hacking through dense jungles. They clear paths. They make trails. They do this faster than other knives. They have many other purposes. They're used for cutting branches and leaves. These branches and leaves could be used for shelter. Machetes are good for digging. They're used to cut down firewood. They're used as weapons. They're used to harvest crops. They're used to cut meat.

SWIM OR SINK?

Black caimans drown their prey. Then, they swallow them.

The El Dorado explorers had to cross the Amazon River. The Amazon River is about 4,000 miles (6,437 km) long. It can flood. It has strong waves. Its waves can sink boats. But the real danger is the creatures living in it.

Black caimans are a type of crocodile. They're about 16 to 20 feet (5 to 6 m) long. They're about 800 to 1,000 pounds (363 to 454 kg). They have strong bites. They can attack big cats. They can attack humans.

The Amazon River fish are also dangerous. Piranhas swim in the river. They have sharp teeth. Electric eels are 6 to 8 feet (1.8 to 2.4 m) long. They shock people. They can cause heart failure. Then, their victims drown.

QUESTION 5

How would you have crossed the Amazon River?

A You were rich. You got workers and enslaved people to build rafts. Rafts are flat structures. They're used to transport people and things. They float. You sat in the middle of the raft.

B You were a worker or an enslaved person. You built the rafts. You also had to work the raft. You used poles to push the rafts across. You were closest to the edge of the raft. You did this several times to get your team across.

C You were poor. Or you were in a hurry to cross. You **waded** across **shallow** water. Wade means to walk through water. Shallow means not deep.

The Amazon River's water is brown.

SURVIVAL RESULTS

Machu Picchu is an ancient Inca site located in the Andes Mountains.

Would you have survived?

Find out! Add up your answers to the chapter questions. Did you have more **A**s, **B**s, or **C**s?

- If you had more **A**s, then you're a survivor! Congrats!

- If you had more **B**s, then you're on the edge. With some luck, you might have just made it.

- If you had more **C**s, then you wouldn't have survived.

Are you happy with your results? Did you have a tie? Sometimes fate is already decided for us. Follow the link below to our webpage. Scroll until you find the series name *Surviving History*. Click download. Print out the template. Follow the directions to create your own paper die. Read the book again. Roll the die to find your new answers. Did your fate change?

https://cherrylakepublishing.com/teaching_guides

DIGGING DEEPER: DID YOU KNOW...?

The search for El Dorado was exciting and dangerous. Many lives were lost. Surviving history involves many different factors. Dig deeper. Consider some of the facts below.

QUESTION 1:

Would you have gone on an expedition?

- Expeditions would head off in any direction. There weren't really maps.
- Expeditions were costly. Most expedition leaders had to borrow money.
- Explorers tried to bribe local people for information.

QUESTION 2:

How would you have protected yourself from the sun?

- Rainforests get about 12 hours of sun a day.
- Rainforest trees grow tall. This is because of sunlight.
- Rainforests are by the **equator**. The equator is the middle of the Earth. The sun's rays directly shine on the equator.

QUESTION 3:

How would you have protected yourself from mosquito bites?

- Not all mosquitoes in the Amazon carry sickness.
- The specific mosquito that carries malaria is more likely to bite at night.
- There are fewer mosquitoes in the dry season. The dry season is June to December.

QUESTION 4:

How would you shelter yourself at night?

- El Dorado explorers were constantly on the move.
- Rainforests are noisy at night. There are lots of animal sounds.
- The rainforest is thick. The ground floor is often dark.

QUESTION 5:

How would you have crossed the Amazon River?

- The Amazon River is a network of hundreds of waterways.
- The Amazon River doesn't have any bridges.
- In the dry season, the Amazon River is 2 to 6 miles (3.2 to 9.7 km) wide. In the wet season, it's 30 miles (48 km) wide.

GLOSSARY

blisters (BLIS-turz) bubbles on the skin
conquered (KAHNG-kurd) took control of
dehydrated (dee-HYE-dray-tid) lacking water
disappeared (dis-uh-PEERD) vanished
enslaved (ehn-SLAYVD) to be owned by another and forced to work for free
equator (ih-KWAY-tur) the middle of the Earth
expeditions (ek-spuh-DISH-uhnz) journeys or adventures with a purpose
hammock (HAM-uhk) hanging bed
humid (HYOO-mid) having a lot of water in the air
legend (LEJ-uhnd) a story that some people believe to be true
nocturnal (nahk-TUR-nuhl) hunting at night

predators (PRED-uh-turz) animals that hunt other animals for food
prey (PRAY) animals that are hunted for food
rainforest (RAYN-for-ist) an area covered with thick trees and with heavy rainfall
shallow (SHAL-oh) not deep
smudge (SMUHJ) a bundle of plants or sticks that burn slowly and produce smoke
starved (STAHRVD) died of hunger
venomous (VEN-uh-muhs) having poison that is injected by fangs
waded (WAYD-id) walked through water

LEARN MORE!

- Aronson, Mark. *Sir Walter Raleigh and the Quest for El Dorado*. New York, NY: Clarion Books, 2000.
- Huey, Lois Miner. *The Search for El Dorado*. New York, NY: Random House, 2016.
- Loh-Hagan, Virginia. *Juliane Koepcke: Lost in Peru*. Ann Arbor, MI: Cherry Lake Publishing, 2018.

INDEX

ABOUT THE AUTHOR

Dr. Virginia Loh-Hagan is an author, university professor, and former classroom teacher. The closest she's been to the Amazon rainforest is Belize. She lives in San Diego with her very tall husband and very naughty dogs. To learn more about her, visit www.virginialoh.com.